The Sister Who Snuck

Autumn Rose Hacker

Archway Publishing books may be ordered through booksellers or by contacting:

Archway Publishing
1663 Liberty Drive
Bloomington, IN 47403
www.archwaypublishing.com
844-669-3957

ISBN: 978-1-4808-9890-5 (sc)
ISBN: 978-1-4808-9891-2 (hc)
ISBN: 978-1-4808-9892-9 (e)

Print information available on the last page.

Archway Publishing rev. date: 06/11/2021

This book is dedicated to my daughters
McKenna and Acadia,
who inspire me every day!

There once was a sister named Sadie,
she was blonde and didn't act like a lady.
She was always in trouble for this or that,
for hitting her sister or stealing her hat.
Sadie didn't care what anyone thought,
she was who she was and in trouble she got.

She'd sneak candy from the cabinets,
cookies from the jar,
paper from the printer
and even the keys for the car.

Her mommy tried and tried to change her as best as she could,
but nothing mommy did helped Sadie be good.

Pretty soon her sister said enough is enough!

You keep hitting me Sadie and it's going to stop.

Stop sneaking around behind mommy's back,

or I'll tell on you always and that will be that.

I've kept your secrets about how you've snuck,

I won't any longer and then you will be stuck.

Sadie hit her sister one last time,

then up came her sister with the drop of a dime.

"Mommy" said her sister yelling through the house.

Sadie always does things and I'm quiet as a mouse.

I can't hold back any longer I say,

this has got to end and it's got to be today!

Those keys that went missing it wasn't your fault,

Sadie took them, they're out in the mulch!

That candy from the cabinet it wasn't me like I said,
it was Sadie who did it when I was in bed.

The cookies in the jar, it wasn't daddy like you thought,

that was Sadie too and she just won't stop!

The paper from your printer you've been wondering about,

wondering about,

it was Sadie mommy I swear, the sister says with a pout.

Mommy looks down at her beautiful curls.

Thank you for telling me you're a good little girl.

Mommy walks to the play room and grabs
Sadie's arm,
looks like your gigs up kid let's go to the yard.
Sadie dug up the keys and told the truth of the rest.

Now Sadie can't sneak because
her sister confessed!

Mommy tucks her girls in at night,

I love you both, you know that right?

She kisses their heads as she hears a grumble,

I'll always love you Sadie even though you like to rumble.

Try hard to be good and we'll get past this someway.

Start with tomorrow, it will be a brand-new day.

Printed in the United States
by Baker & Taylor Publisher Services